D1237891

World of Farming

Provided as a generous gift of the Orange County Library Foundation

Jobs on a Farm

Nancy Dickmann

www.raintreepublishers.co.uk
Visit our website to find out
more information about
Raintree books.

To order:
☎ Phone 0845 6044371
🖹 Fax +44 (0) 1865 312263
🖥 Email myorders@raintreepublishers.co.uk

Customers from outside the UK please telephone +44 1865 312262

Raintree is an imprint of Capstone Global Library Limited, a company incorporated in England and Wales having its registered office at 7 Pilgrim Street, London, EC4V 6LB – Registered company number: 6695582

Edited by Siân Smith, Nancy Dickmann, and Rebecca Rissman
Designed by Joanna Hinton-Malivoire
Picture research by Mica Brancic
Production by Victoria Fitzgerald
Originated by Capstone Global Library Ltd
Colour reproduction by Dot Gradations Ltd, UK
Printed and bound in China by South China Printing Company Ltd

ISBN 978 0 431 19556 8
15 14 13 12 11
10 9 8 7 6 5 4 3 2 1

British Library Cataloguing in Publication Data
Dickmann, Nancy.
Jobs on a farm. -- (World of farming)
1. Farm life--Pictorial works--Juvenile literature.
I. Title II. Series
630-dc22

Acknowledgements
We would like to thank the following for permission to reproduce photographs: Photolibrary pp.**4** (Comstock/Creatas), **5** (Botanica/Aaron McCoy), **6** (Britain on View/Rod Edwards), **7** (Fresh Food Images/Gerrit Buntrock), **8** (Japan Travel Bureau), **9** (Blend Images RF/Karin Dreyer), **10** (White), **11** (imagebroker.net/Konrad Wothe), **12** (Imagebroker.net/Jim West), **13** (Nordic Photos/Sven Rosenhall), **15** (age fotostock/Jordi Cami), **16** (imagebroker.net/ulrich niehoff), **17** (Tao Images Limited), **18** (Corbis), **19** (Brand X Pictures/Jupiter Images), **20** (Design Pics Inc/Leah Warkentin), **21** (imagebroker.net/Ernst Wrba), **22** (Blend Images RF/Karin Dreyer), **23 top** (Brand X Pictures/Jupiter Images), **23 middle top** (imagebroker.net/ulrich niehoff), **23 middle bottom** (imagebroker.net/Ernst Wrba); Shutterstock pp.**14** (Chepko Danil Vitalevich), **23 bottom** (Chepko Danil Vitalevich).

Front cover photograph of a man pouring grain into a feeder for (miniature) Hereford calves reproduced with permission of iStockPhoto (© emholk). Back cover photograph of strawberry fields being watered in Thailand reproduced with permission of Photolibrary (age fotostock/Jordi Cami).

The publisher would like to thank Dee Reid, Diana Bentley, and Nancy Harris for their invaluable help with this book.

Contents

What is a farm?

A farm is a place where food is grown.

There are many different jobs on farms.

Caring for animals

Some farmers keep animals.

Some farmers milk cows.

wool

Some farmers cut wool.

Some farmers collect eggs.

Farmers feed their animals every day.

Farmers help their animals to stay healthy.

Growing plants

lettuce

Some farmers grow plants for us to eat.

They get the land ready for planting.

seeds

They plant seeds.

They water plants to help them grow.

They spread manure to help
plants grow.

They pick the plants when they are
ready to eat.

Running the farm

Farmers take care of farm buildings.

Farmers clear out barns.

Farmers take care of their
farm machines.

Farmers sell their food at markets.

Can you remember?

What do farmers collect
from chickens?

Answer on page 24

Picture glossary

 **barn** farm building where animals live. Farmers also keep hay or farm machines in barns.

 **manure** most manure is made from animal poo. It helps plants to grow.

 **market** place where things can be bought and sold. Many farmers sell food at markets.

 **seed** plants grow from seeds. Farmers plant seeds in the ground.

Index

Answer to quiz on page 22: Farmers collect eggs from chickens.

Notes to parents and teachers
Before reading
Ask the children if they have ever visited a farm. Ask them what different jobs they think people do on a farm. Would they like to do any of these jobs? Are there any jobs they wouldn't want to do?

After reading
• Read *Farmer Duck* by Martin Waddell to the class. Then re-read the story and get the children to act out all the different jobs that the duck has to do. They can join in every time the farmer calls out 'How goes the work?' Then get them to act out the cow, sheep, and hens creeping into the farmhouse and waking up the farmer.

• Ask children to mime different jobs on a farm and see if the others can guess what they are doing.